ACKNOWLEDGMENTS

Designed and illustrated by Mei Lim
Photographs by Peter Millard

Created by Thumbprint Books

Library of Congress Cataloging-in-Publication Data

Gayle, Katie.
  Snappy, jazzy jewelry / by Katie Gayle.
      p.   cm.
  Originally published under title: Snappy, jazzy jewellery. Hamlyn Ltd., c1994.
  Includes index.
  ISBN 0-8069-3854-4
  1. Jewelry making.   I. Gayle, Katie. Snappy, jazzy jewellery.   II. Title.
TT212.G39   1995
745.594'2—dc20   95-21848
                                                                           CIP

2   4   6   8   10   9   7   5   3   1

Published 1995 by Sterling Publishing Company, Inc.
387 Park Avenue South, New York, N.Y. 10016
Originally published in Great Britain by Hamlyn Children's Books
Part of Reed International Books
© 1995 Thumbprint Books
Distributed in Canada by Sterling Publishing
c/o Canadian Manda Group, One Atlantic Avenue, Suite 105
Toronto, Ontario, Canada M6K 3E7
Printed and bound in Italy

Sterling   ISBN 0-8069-3854-4

SNAPPY JAZZY JEWELRY

CONTENTS

KATIE GAYLE

JACQUELINE RUSSON

Sterling Publishing Co., Inc. New York

Making your own jewelry

It's hard to believe that all the fabulous pieces of jewelry in this book are made from things that are easily found around the house, in the garden, in the sewing basket and even in the tool box. Most of them can be made using everyday household tools. The only special tools you may need are two pairs of pliers—a pair of round-nose pliers, which are useful for bending and shaping wire and metal, and a pair of needle-nose pliers, which you use for holding things in place. You can buy them cheaply from a hardware store or craft shop.

PAINT

You can use either acrylic or poster paints to decorate your jewelry. Acrylic paints leave a shiny finish. If you use poster paints instead, you may want to varnish your pieces. Use a clear, waterproof varnish or clear nail varnish.

SAFETY TIPS

• When cutting with a sharp knife, always cut away from your body.

• Use a metal file to file off any sharp edges or corners.

• Be careful when you use a needle or knitting needle to poke a hole through thick paper, cork or tinfoil. Hold the object on a firm surface while you make the hole.

• Always use strong glue and varnish in a well-ventilated room and ask an adult to help you.

knitting needles

rug hook

brushes

scissors

file

round-nose pliers

tweezers

kitchen knife

needle-nose pliers

Findings

These are the names of the findings you will need to make the pieces of jewelry in this book.

jump rings

gold and silver beads

lapel pins

fish-hooks for pierced ears

bell cups

posts

clip-on earring backs

necklace clasps

necklet ends

cuff link fittings

brooch backs

beading thread

head pins

plastic-coated wire

bracelet clasps

screw eye

spacing bars

ring blank

metal wire

barrette clips

GLUE

For most of the jewelry, you will need strong glue to bond things together. There are glues that are recommended especially for metal, plastic, fabric or paper. Before you begin, read the instructions carefully on how to use each kind.

hammer

awl

end nipper

Special Techniques

MAKING HOLES FOR TIN BRACELET

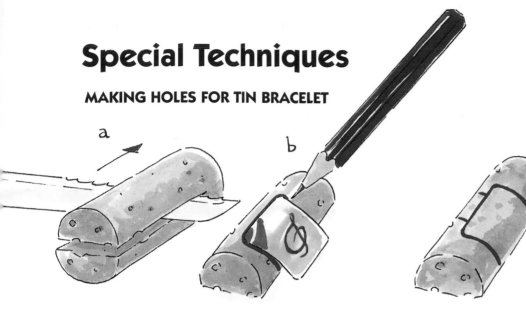

1 Use a serrated knife to cut a cork in half lengthways (a). Trace half of one of the tin shapes on the cork (b).

2 Draw two short marker lines on the cork at equal distances from two corners of the tin shape, like this.

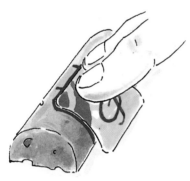

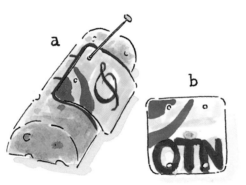

3 Fit a tin shape exactly into the drawn shape on the cork and hold it down firmly.

4 Use a pin to make two holes in the tin, about 1/16 inch from the edge, using the two short marker lines as guides (a). Do the same on the opposite edge (b)

MAKING PAPER PULP

Tear some newspaper into strips (a). Put them in an old bowl and soak them in plenty of hot water for several hours, stirring from time to time. When the paper is mushy, scoop it out of the bowl and squeeze out any extra water (b). If you store the pulp in a plastic container with a lid, it will last for a long time (c).

BLANKET STITCH

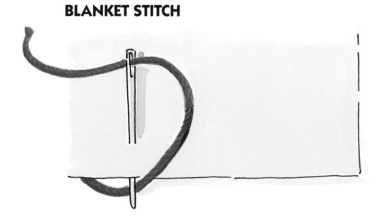

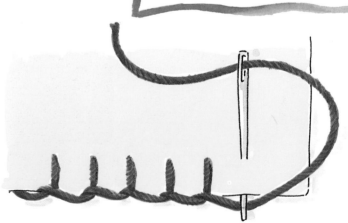

1 Work from left to right with the thread or wool at the bottom edge of the fabric. Point the needle downwards and push it through the fabric from front to back, like this.

2 Pull the thread out between the fabric and the thread, as shown. Do this again and again until you have sewn along the edges of the fabric shape. Try not to pull the thread too tight.

STRINGING BEADS

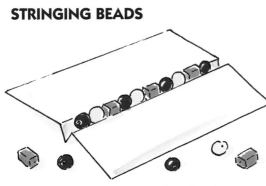

1 Make a pleat in the middle of a piece of paper, as shown. Open out the pleat and arrange your beads in the order you want to string them to make your necklace or bracelet .

2 Cut a piece of nylon wire or beading thread at least twice as long as the length of your necklace. Feed three beads on to the thread, leaving about 2 inches hanging free.

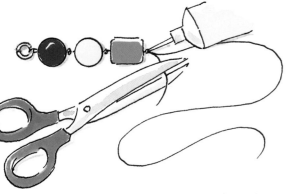

3 Thread on a jump ring and then feed the thread back through the last bead. Tie a knot. Feed the thread through the second bead and tie a knot and then through the third. Secure the knots with a drop of glue.

4 Continue feeding beads onto the thread. When you have threaded them all, add a jump ring in the same way as you did at the beginning. Fix a necklace or bracelet catch onto the jump rings.

FOIL BEADS

Scrunch a piece of silver foil into a ball and roll it in the palm of your hand (a). Cover it with colored foil (b). Push a pin or nail through the bead to make a hole (c).

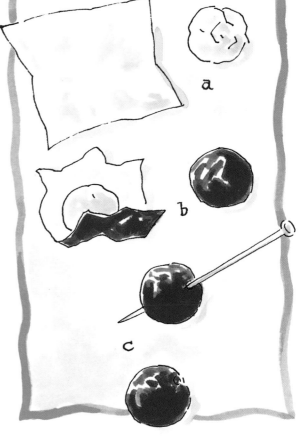

MAKING A FLAT SPIRAL

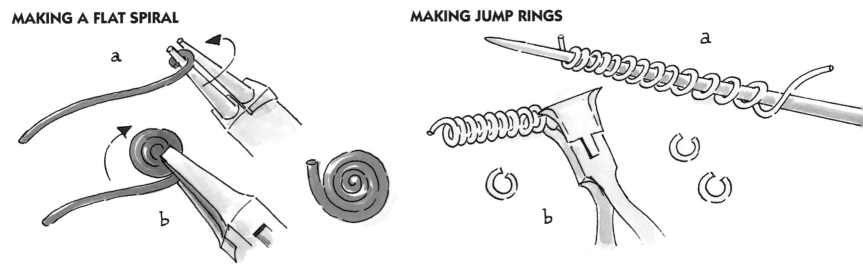

Cut a length of wire. Using the tip of a pair of round-nose pliers, twist one end of the wire into a small loop (a). Hold the loop with a pair of needle-nose pliers and turn the wire around and around to make a flat spiral (b).

MAKING JUMP RINGS

To make your own jump rings, wind a length of wire around a knitting needle, pushing the spirals close together as you wind (a). Pull the wire spiral off the needle and cut through it with end nippers, as shown (b).

Something from Nothing

Turn tin cans, aluminum containers, plastic bottles, corks, pencils and plastic shopping bags into beautiful brooches, earrings and necklaces. Look around your house to see what else you can recycle to create magnificent pieces of jewelry.

CRINKLE CRANKLE EARRINGS

For each earring, cut out the corrugated side from a clean foil food container. Round off one end and snip zig-zags in the other end. Pierce a hole close to the top of the rounded end. Glue a spiral of colored wire onto an ear fitting. Thread the end of the wire through the hole in the ear fitting, a small washer and the hole in the foil shape. Loop the end of the wire to hold it in place.

PLASTIC PETAL EARRINGS

Cut 24 petal shapes from a colorful plastic bag. Thread an ear fitting through the center of 12 petals. Do the same to the other 12. Push a bell cup and a small bead over each earring. Fix them in place with a dab of glue.

PRETTY PLEATED EARRINGS

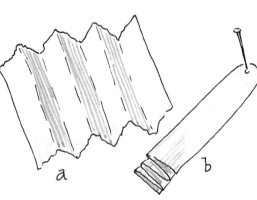

1 For each earring, cut a rectangle, about 2 x 4 inches, from the side of a foil container. Pleat it, as shown (a). Round off one end. Pierce a hole through the top of the pleats with a pin (b).

2 Make a foil bead (see page 9). Thread a length of wire through the bead (c) and make a loop at each end of the wire (d). Thread one loop through the holes in the pleated foil. Fix an ear fitting to the other loop. Fan out the pleats (e).

CRAZY CORK EARRINGS

1 Cut a cork in half with a serrated knife. Paint both halves gold or silver (a). Twist a small brass screw eye onto the top of each cork half, as shown, and attach an ear fitting (b).

2 Make two heart shapes out of thin colored wire (c). Glue one to the flat side of each cork earring. Fit shiny paper inside each heart. Make two wire spirals (see page 9) and push one into the bottom of each earring (d).

SHINY SPIRAL EARRINGS

Cut the base of a foil food container into a square. Glue colored foil wrap to the top. Cut it into strips, each about ⅜ x 4 inches. Wrap each strip around a pencil to make a spiral. Make a hole at one end and fix on an ear fitting.

NYLON NETTING EARRINGS

Cut two pieces of netting, each about 1½ inches wide. Wind embroidery thread tightly around one end of each piece. Secure it with a drop of glue. Fit a jump ring and an ear fitting onto each one.

13

FABULOUS FOIL BROOCH

1 Press some clean silver foil into a measuring spoon, as shown, to make a dome (a). Color it with acrylic paint (b). Let the paint dry.

2 Place the dome on stiff cardboard and draw around it. Add zig-zags, as shown, and cut out the card shape (a). Paint it on one side (b). Let it dry.

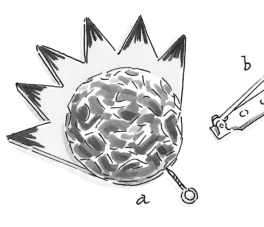

3 Glue the dome to the card shape. Fit a small screw eye into the bottom of the dome (a). Glue a brooch back on the back of the card (b).

4 Make a foil bead (see page 9). Fit it on a jump ring and hang it on the screw eye on the bottom of the brooch.

PLASTIC BOTTLE BRACELET

Cut a strip, about 1¼ inches wide, from a clean, clear plastic soft-drink bottle. Trim the edges. Decorate the outside with colorful stickers or sticky labels.

PENCIL BROOCH

Glue two or three small pencils together with strong glue. Leave them to dry. Tie them together with colored string. Hang small objects from the string. Glue on a brooch back.

14

MEDAL BROOCH

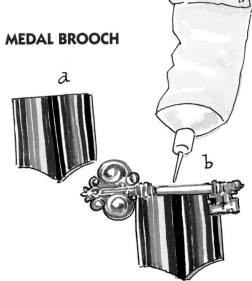

1 Glue a piece of striped ribbon onto stiff cardboard. When it is firmly stuck, cut it into the shape shown (a). Glue a key across the straight edge of the ribbon (b).

2 Glue a strip of tape down the middle of the back of the card (c). Let it dry. Glue a bow, bead and chocolate coin on the front of the tape (d). Glue on a brooch back.

THIN TIN BRACELET

Wash out a used aluminum can. Ask an adult to cut off the top and bottom with scissors. Trim the edges and cut out five or six 1¼-inch tin squares. File them smooth. Round off the edges. Pierce four holes in each tin square (see page 8). Hook the squares together with jump rings. Fit a catch on the ends of the bracelet.

SCRUNCHY PLASTIC BRACELET

Cut a strip, 1¼ inches wide and 30 inches long, from a plastic bag. Cut zig-zags along both long edges. Make nine or ten chocolate wrapper beads (see page 9). Thread a needle with thin elastic. Make four pleats at one end of the plastic strip. Push the needle through the middle of the pleats. Feed on a chocolate foil wrapper bead. Repeat this until you reach the end of the strip. Knot the ends of the elastic and secure the knot with a drop of glue.

It's only natural

You don't have to search far to find the things you need to make this natty natural jewelry. Just look in the garden, on the beach, in the woods and around the house. Remember that all the pieces shown here are inspirational. You can use whatever leaves, flowers, nuts and seeds you want.

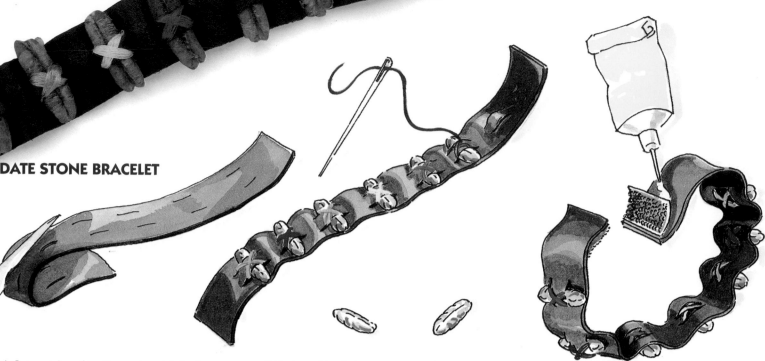

DATE STONE BRACELET

1 Cut a strip of leather, about 8 inches long and 1 inch wide. Cut seven double-slits, each about ½ inch long, at equal distances in the leather. It is easier to cut the slits by bending the leather over, as shown.

2 Push a dried date stone under each leather strip. Sew each stone in place with a different colored embroidery thread. Start at the back of the stone and criss-cross the thread over the leather strip, like this.

3 Cut a small piece of velcro. Separate the two halves. Glue the rough half on the top of one end of the bracelet. Glue the furry half to the underneath of the other end.

BAY LEAF BEAUTIES

Paint two bay leaves or other flexible green leaves with acrylic paint. When the paint is dry, glue tiny stars, seeds or beads all over each leaf. When the glue is dry, press the leaves between heavy books to flatten them. Thread two beads onto each stalk. Pierce an earring fitting through the stalk just above the beads.

PERFECT PEBBLE CUFF LINKS

Find some small smooth pebbles or colored stones. Fit each of them into a cuff link fitting. If they are not quite flat, secure them on the metal plate with a drop of glue. Bend the metal claws over the pebbles.

ORANGE PEEL NECKLACE

Score the peel of an orange or tangerine into quarters with a sharp knife. Carefully pull them off the orange. Cut each quarter into three or four petal shapes. Remove any thick pith. Pierce a hole in the top of each petal.

Bake the petals in a low oven for 30 minutes. If you want brown petals, bake them for longer. Fit a jump ring through each petal hole. Thread a leather thong through the jump ring of one petal. Add five beads. Continue doing this until you have used seven petals, as shown. Put a big bead on to either end of the necklace. Secure them with knots.

DAINTY DROP EARRINGS

To make these dainty earrings, use flowers and fruits, such as physalis, that have paper-like pods. Paint the pods and remove any stalks. Push a long pin through the pod, then through a pearl and a small gold bead. Loop the end of the pin. Attach an ear fitting onto the loop.

NUTTY LAPEL PIN

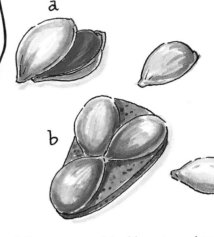

1 Open some pistachio nuts and remove the nuts (a). Glue three half shells in the pattern shown onto a piece of old cork tile or thick cardboard (b).

2 Paint the shells. When they are dry, cut off any extra cork tile or cardboard. File the edges smooth with an emery board.

3 Glue on a pearl or bead and some small feathers, as shown. Highlight the shells with gold paint. Glue a lapel pin fitting onto the back.

NATURAL NECKLACE

1 Pierce a hole through the stalks or stems of feathers, rosehips, cones, dried leaves, seeds and other natural things. Fit on jump rings. Close the rings.

2 Thread a thin flexible twig, about 5 inches long, through all the jump rings. With colored thread, bind the ends of the twig to keep the jump rings from falling off.

3 Cut a length of cord long enough to loop over your head. Tie it to each end of the twig, as shown. Secure the knots with glue.

SIMPLE STONE BROOCH

Find three small, smooth oval stones. Glue a brooch pin onto the back of the biggest one. Wind colored thread tightly around the middle of the stone and over the brooch pin. Wind different colored threads around the other two stones.

Attach the stones by sewing the threads loosely together, as shown. Wind a contrasting colored thread around and around the joins. Secure it with a knot.

TREE BARK BARRETTE

Paint gold highlights on the rough side of a piece of tree bark. Glue a barrette onto the smoothest side. To make your barrette more decorative, glue on sequins and shiny beads.

POPPY-HEAD EARRINGS

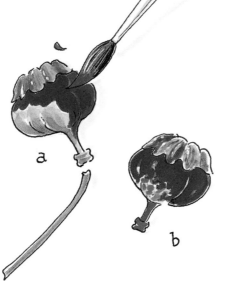

1 Paint two dried poppy heads blue and gold (a). Trim their stalks (b).

2 To make tassels, wind red thread around and around a small piece of cardboard (a). Slide the thread off the card. Leaving a small loop, wind a length of thread tightly around one end of the tassel threads, as shown (b). Knot the end.

3 Cut the loop at the other end of the threads to make tassel fringes (a). Fit a jump ring through the tassel loop (b).

4 Twist a screw eye into the top and bottom of the poppy head. Dab on glue to fix them. Attach the tassel and an earring fitting, as shown.

SNAZZY SHELL BROOCH

Glue small colorful feathers to the wide end of a sliced shell (which you can buy in a shell shop). Glue a cluster of shells on top. If you have a shell with a hole in it, you can hang another shell from it with two jump rings. Glue a brooch pin to the back of the sliced shell.

PERFECT PAPER JEWELS

It's simple to make these vibrant and exciting pieces of jewelry from scraps of white, brown, tissue or crêpe paper. Add a touch of paint to create earrings, necklaces and other pieces that everyone will notice.

GLITTERY GOLD EARRINGS

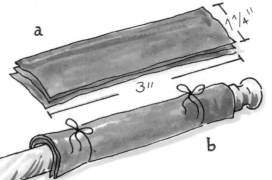

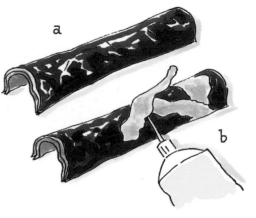

1 Tear brown paper into six rectangles, each about 1¼ x 3 inches. Glue three pieces one on top of the other (a). Mold them around a wooden spoon handle, tying them in place with string (b).

2 Glue a piece of colored foil over the outside curve (a). Glue small pieces of gold paper on top, leaving some of the foil showing, like this (b).

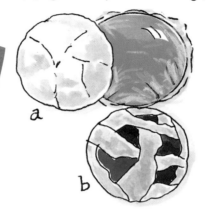

3 Make a dome of layered white paper strips, using a round button covered with plastic wrap, as a mold (a). When it is dry, cover the circle with colored foil and gold paper as shown above (b).

4 Pierce a hole in both parts of each earring, as shown (see Making holes in tin on page 8). Fit a jump ring through both holes to join the two parts together. Glue an ear fitting on to the back of the dome.

CRÊPE CUFF LINKS

For each cuff link, cut three strips of metallic crêpe paper in two different colors. Roll each strip tightly around a toothpick. Glue down the end before you remove the toothpick. Cut a ½-inch square of cardboard. Cover it with crêpe paper. Glue on the three paper rolls in a staggered line, as shown. Glue a cuff link fitting to the back.

SHOOTING STAR BROOCH

Cut a star shape out of cardboard. Glue several layers of paper strips on one side. Use tissue paper for the final layer. Leave the star to dry before painting both sides. Soak 12 inches of string in hot water. Spread glue over the tissue paper on the star. Press the wet string into the glue in a spiral. Paint it when it has dried. Glue a brooch pin onto the back.

SUNBURST RING

Make a round, flat shape in paper pulp (see page 8). When it is dry, cover it with two layers of white tissue paper. Glue on some long seeds, all pointing towards the center. Cover them with two more layers of tissue. Glue a small ball of paper pulp in the center. Paint the bead and the circle in contrasting colors. Highlight the seeds with gold. Glue a ring blank on the back.

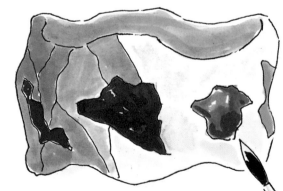

ROLLED PAPER NECKLACE

Cut thin triangles and rectangular strips of thick white paper, all about 12 inches long. Paint both edges of each strip, using a fine brush or a toothpick. When the paint is dry, roll each strip over a toothpick to make beads. Glue down the end. Remove the toothpicks and string the beads together to make an unusual necklace.

CRINKLE CRANKLE BANGLE

2"

10"

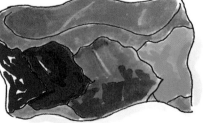

1 Cut two wavy lengths of cardboard, 2 x 10 inches, and glue them together. Bend the card into a bangle. Overlap the ends and glue them together. Glue layers of paper strips on both sides. On the outer side, stick on scraps of colored foil.

2 Glue torn pieces of brown paper to the outside of the bangle. Leave flashes of foil showing, like this. Cover the inside of the bangle with brown paper. Paint all the brown paper pieces silver.

PAPER-BEAD NECKLACE

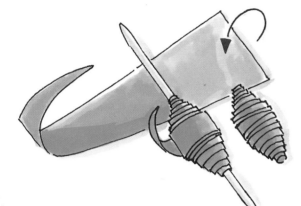

1 Make 19 rolled paper beads (see Rolled paper necklace on page 25). Use green paper triangles instead of white paper with painted edges.

2 Make 18 round beads out of pulp paper (see page 8) and let them dry completely.

3 Cover each pulp bead with a layer of thin tissue paper (a). When they are dry, paint the beads. Let the paint dry (b).

4 Push a screw eye into each bead. String them alternately with the rolled paper beads, as shown. Leave enough string to tie around your neck.

ELABORATE EARRINGS

For each earring, cut out a triangular shape and a half-circle shape, as shown, from a piece of stiff cardboard. Glue strips of paper all over each shape. To create a smooth surface, glue a layer of white tissue paper on top.

Use an awl or nail to pierce a hole in the triangular shape and another in the half-circle, as shown. Paint both shapes and let them dry. Fit the shapes together with three jump rings. Glue an earring fitting on the back of each half-circle.

PULP-PAPER RINGS

Press some paper pulp (see page 8) into a small, star-shaped cookie cutter. Gently remove it and let it dry. Glue two layers of thin white paper over the pulp star. When it is dry, paint the star and glue on colored stones or beads. Glue a ring blank to the back. You can make all sorts of different shapes by hand or with cookie-cutters.

SMILING SUN BROOCH

Cut a sun shape out of stiff card-board. For the face, glue a dome of pulp paper in the center and let it dry. Glue a layer of thin tissue paper all over the sun shape. When it is dry, paint it yellow and decorate it with a smiling face and colorful sunbursts.

TIGER BROOCH

Make some paper pulp (see page 8). Press the pulp into a big, heart-shaped cookie cutter. Gently remove it and let it dry. Glue several layers of yellow tissue paper all over the pulp heart. Tear strips of black tissue paper and glue them onto the yellow tissue, as shown, to make a striped pattern. Glue a brooch fitting to the back.

CURLY CARD BARRETTE

Cut out this shape from stiff cardboard. Glue a layer of paper pulp (see page 8) to one side and let it dry. Then glue a layer of white tissue paper all over the cardboard shape. When it is dry, paint a colorful pattern on the tissue paper. Decorate the front with flat beads or shiny sequins. Glue a barrette to the back.

CLAY CREATIONS

Clay is fun to work with because it is easy to roll, knead, press and pinch into any shape you choose, to make unusual and stunning pieces of jewelry like these. You can use either self-hardening clay and paint it, or oven-hardening clay, which comes in all sorts of bright colors.

JAZZY RINGS

Make long thin sausages of colored oven-baked clay. For each ring, cut a length long enough to fit around a finger. Press the ends together to make a ring shank. Make a clay star, heart, spiral or any other shape you like to put on top. Bake the shape and the shank flat in the oven. When they are cool and hard, glue the shape onto the ring shank.

LADYBUG EARRINGS

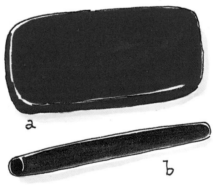

FLOWERY EARRINGS

Press two balls of self-hardening clay into flat circles. Pinch pleats in them to make them look like flower petals, as shown. Make two small clay spirals. When the clay has hardened, paint each petal a different color and add spots in other colors. Paint the spirals red. Glue a spiral on the center of each painted flower and an earring fitting on the back.

1 Roll out a flat rectangle of red oven-baked clay, about ⅛-inch thick (a). Make a log of black oven-baked clay, about ¼-inch in diameter (b).

2 Wrap the red rectangle around the black log and roll them together evenly (a). Trim the rough ends and then cut the rest into ¼-inch sections (b).

3 For each earring, press eight sections together to make a long ladybug shape. Make two black antennae and press them onto one end of the ladybug. Pierce a hole in the center of the same end.

4 Bake the ladybugs on a metal tray until they are hard. When they are cool, fit a jump ring through each hole. Add another jump ring and then attach an ear fitting, as shown.

TWIRLY-WHIRLY NECKLACE

Roll out three long lengths of oven-baked clay, in contrasting colors, and press them side by side. Twist one end in one direction and the other end in the opposite direction to make a long spiral of colors. Roll the twisted length on a flat surface to press the colors firmly together. Cut it into two.

Roll each length again to make both of them even longer. Taper the ends. Make each one into a twirly shape, as shown, and bake them in the oven. Knot them onto a cord, long enough to tie around your neck.

HEART BROOCH

Roll some self-hardening clay flat on a piece of rough fabric. Either use a heart template or cookie cutter to shape a clay heart. Make a spiral of clay, as shown. Leave it to harden and then paint it gold. Paint the heart red. Add specks of gold when the paint is dry. Glue the spiral to the painted side of the heart and a brooch pin on to the back.

TINGLE-TANGLE BRACELET

1 Make several small shapes out of self-hardening clay. Make them by hand, use cookie cutters or press shells or metal shapes into the clay.

2 Make a hole in each shape with a toothpick while the clay is soft (a). When the clay is dry, smooth any rough bits with an emery board (b). Paint the shapes in bright colors (c).

3 Make nine clay spiral beads, as shown (a). Leave them to harden and then paint them (b).

4 Cut a length of round elastic long enough to fit around your wrist plus a little extra. Fit a jump ring to each shape. Thread alternate shapes and spirals on the elastic. Knot the ends of the elastic and hide the knot under one of the spirals.

SPIRAL HAIR COMB

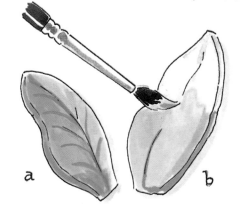

1 Roll out a length of self-hardening clay, about 10 inches long. Taper it at both ends (a). Curl each end into a spiral (b).

2 Lay the twirly shape over the side of a straight-sided glass, a rolling pin or a tin, as shown. Let it harden and then paint it.

STARFISH EARRINGS

Shape two small starfish from self-hardening clay. While they are still wet, prick them all over with a toothpick, as shown. Leave the starfish to harden and then paint them. When the paint is dry, glue an earring fitting to the back of each one.

3 Make two leaves with fine veins from self-hardening clay (a). When they are hard, paint them green (b).

4 Glue the twirly shape and the leaves on a hair comb with a flat, wide top.

LADYBUG LEAF BROOCH

Roll out a ball of green oven-baked clay until it is about ⅛ inch thick. Press tiny bits of yellow clay into the green and roll it flat again. Cut the clay into the shape of a leaf. Mark on veins with a toothpick.

For the ladybug, make an oval shape with a flat bottom out of red oven-baked clay. Press on a black clay head and spots. Press the ladybug onto the leaf and put them in the oven to join and harden. When they are cool, glue to a brooch back.

TERRA-COTTA BEAD BRACELET

Roll five oval-shaped beads from terra-cotta colored self-hardening clay. With a wooden skewer or knitting needle, poke a hole through each bead. Leave the skewer in place as you press the sides and ends of each bead with the palm of your hand to make it rectangular. Let the beads harden.

Make five smaller, flatter beads and poke a hole through each one. Let them harden and then paint them gold. Thread the beads, first a big one and then a gold one, as shown, onto rounded elastic. Knot the ends.

CLEVER CLAY NECKLACE

Make several round, oval- and lozenge-shaped beads from self-hardening clay. With a thin knitting needle or skewer, poke a hole through each bead.

While they are still wet, make patterns on the beads with a toothpick. Let the beads harden and then paint them different colors with acrylic paint. Thread string, long enough to tie around your neck, through the beads.

PRESSED CUFF LINKS

Roll two small balls of self-hardening clay. While they are still soft, press a seed head or a shell into the middle of each ball and then gently pull it away. You will see that the seed head or shell has left a pattern in the clay.

Let the clay shapes harden and then paint them green with gold highlights. Glue a cuff-link fitting to the back of each painted shape.

HEAVY METAL

These ingenious pieces of jewelry are all made from bits of metal—scraps of wire, dog tags, washers, nuts, old hangers, nails, tiny springs and paper fasteners. Raid the family tool box to see what other metal things you can find.

COPPER NAIL NECKLACE

Push several small copper nails through a colored shoelace. Hammer the pointed ends flat. Flatten them one by one on something hard and unbreakable.

HORSE SHOE NAIL BROOCH

Cut some old rubber or thick leather into a half-circle, as shown. Glue on several horse shoe nails, washers and a colorful plastic stone or bead. Glue on a brooch back.

TWISTED-WIRE NECKLACE

Wrap a long piece of copper wire tightly around a knitting needle. Remove the needle and stretch, twist and fold back the wire, as shown. Attach jump rings to the wire and hang small metal objects from each one. Add a metal ring to each end of the necklace. Attach string or shoelaces to the rings to tie around your neck.

DOG TAG NECKLACE

1 Cut the hook and sides off a metal coat hanger with metal cutters (a). Shape the hanger into a circle around a paint can (b).

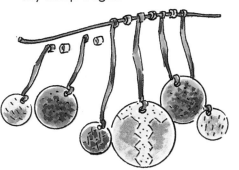

2 Bend the ends into hooks and hammer them flat. File and sandpaper any sharp edges.

3 Use a nail to punch and scratch patterns on different-sized dog tags. Thread a piece of copper wire through each tag. Hammer the wires flat.

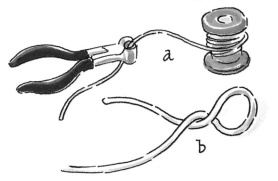

4 Loop the ends of the flattened wires around a length of copper wire. Add a washer inbetween each one. Attach the necklace wire to the hanger hooks.

JANGLE BANGLE

1 Wind copper tape or metallic sticky tape around a wooden curtain ring.

2 Cut five lengths of soft wire, each about 6 inches long (a). Twist a loop on one end of each length, as shown (b).

3 Wind each length around the bracelet, leaving the loops free and the loose end tucked under, like this.

4 Hang a small metal object on a jump ring from each of the loops.

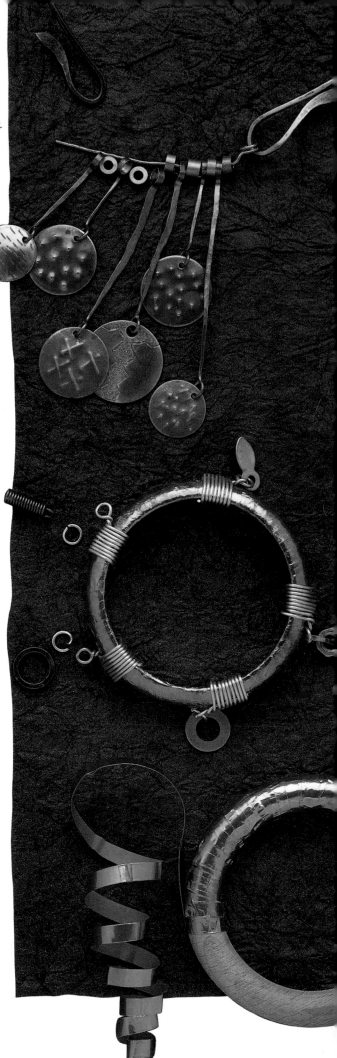

STUDDED LEATHER BRACELET

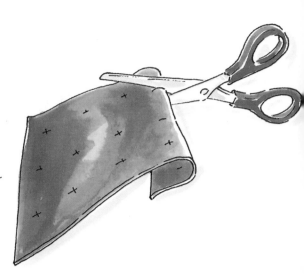

1 Measure around your wrist and around your arm, below your elbow. Use these measurements to cut out a piece of soft leather in this shape, which fits comfortably around your arm.

2 Make marks at equal distances on the leather. Cut ⅛-inch slits with scissors. Bend the leather as you cut each slit, which should be no wider than a paper fastener.

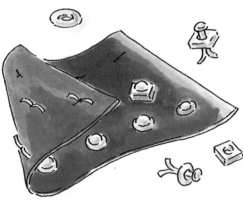

3 Push a paper fastener through a nut or washer and then through one of the slits in the leather. Bend the ends flat at the back to keep it in place. Decorate each slit in the same way.

4 Punch holes at equal distances down the two long edges of the leather. Glue a small washer over each hole. Thread a shoelace through the holes, as shown.

NUTS AND WASHERS

To make these earrings, cuff links and rings, glue colorful stones onto the centers of large, chunky nuts or round, domed washers. Glue each nut or washer onto a ring, ear fitting or cuff link. A matching set of earrings and a ring makes a good present.

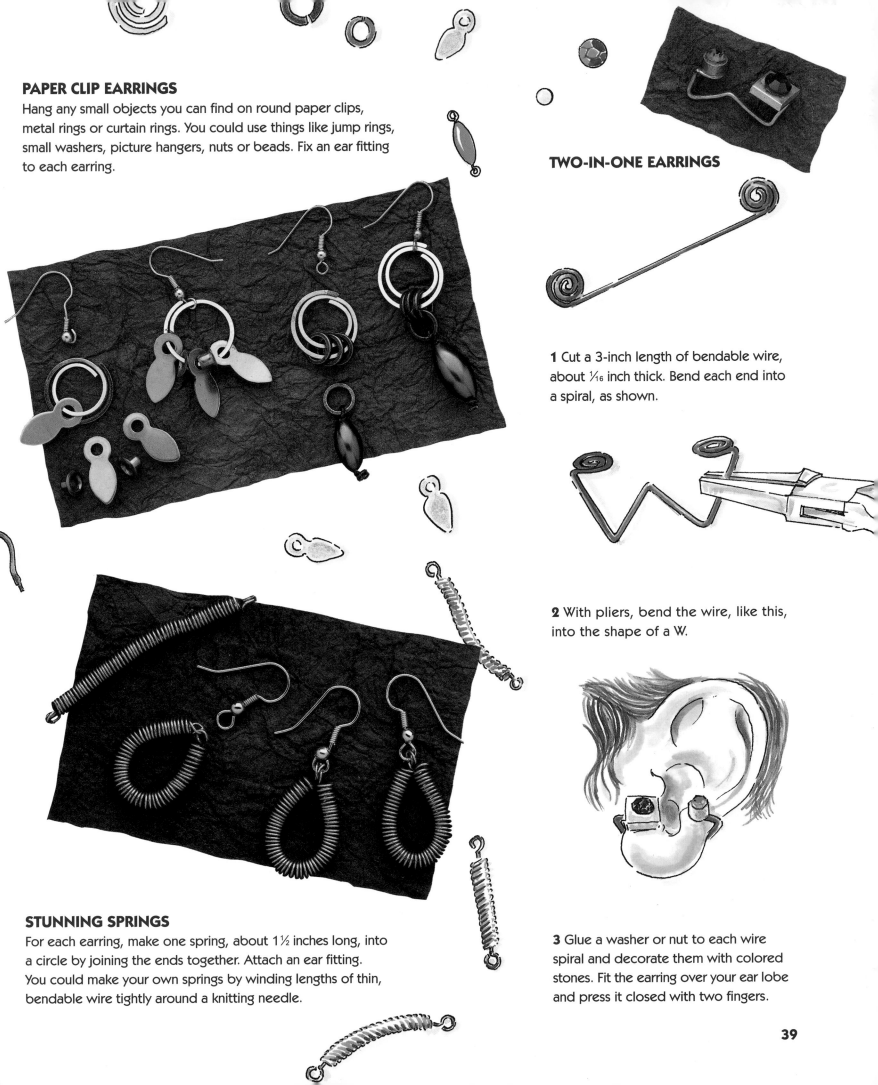

PAPER CLIP EARRINGS

Hang any small objects you can find on round paper clips, metal rings or curtain rings. You could use things like jump rings, small washers, picture hangers, nuts or beads. Fix an ear fitting to each earring.

TWO-IN-ONE EARRINGS

1 Cut a 3-inch length of bendable wire, about ¹⁄₁₆ inch thick. Bend each end into a spiral, as shown.

2 With pliers, bend the wire, like this, into the shape of a W.

STUNNING SPRINGS

For each earring, make one spring, about 1½ inches long, into a circle by joining the ends together. Attach an ear fitting. You could make your own springs by winding lengths of thin, bendable wire tightly around a knitting needle.

3 Glue a washer or nut to each wire spiral and decorate them with colored stones. Fit the earring over your ear lobe and press it closed with two fingers.

39

BUTTONS AND BOWS

Don't throw away any scraps of ribbon, fabric, wool or embroidery thread. It's easy to combine them with buttons, beads and sequins from the sewing box to make these unusual and eye-catching pieces of jewelry.

SHINY BOW TIE

1 Sew or glue shiny sequins onto an old bow tie. If you don't have one, you can make your own bow tie from a long strip of felt or some stiff, wide ribbon.

2 Sew the bow tie to the middle of a length of colored elastic long enough to fit around your neck, with a little over-lapping (a). Sew on velcro (b).

BEADY BRACELET

Thread a needle with a very long piece of embroidery thread. Wind the embroidery thread seven times around a wooden curtain ring. Then thread on a tiny, colorful bead, as shown. Keep doing this until you have covered the wooden ring with embroidery thread and beads. Glue the end down with a dab of glue.

GLORIOUS GLASS-BEAD CHOKER

Cut a length of velvet ribbon long enough to fit around your neck, plus a little overlapping. Sew sequins and gold beads onto the ribbon. Hang glass beads from the bottom edge of the ribbon. Cut a small piece of velcro. Separate the two halves. Sew the rough half on the top of one end of the ribbon. Sew the other half to the underneath of the other end.

WOOLY BEAD HAIRBAND

1 Cut 15 strands of colorful wool, each about 30 inches long. Divide them into three groups of five strands each. To each group, add a long strand of colorful beads.

2 Tie or knot the strands together at one end and make a long braid. When you get to the end, knot or tie the ends and cut off any extra wool or beads.

3 Cut a piece of wide black elastic, about 4 inches long. Sew it onto the inside of the braid, as shown.

GLITTERING EARRINGS

For each earring, cut a strip of see-through fabric, about 5 inches long and 2 inches wide. Fold the strip in half, widthways. Sew the sides together and fill the pouch with shiny sequins and scraps of shiny fabric. Bind the open end of the pouch with gold thread. Fit a jump ring with an earring fitting through the thread.

BRIGHT BUTTON EARRINGS

Decorate two big buttons with fabric paint. Let the paint dry. Glue a clip earring fitting to the back of each button. Let them dry. Make two tassels with gold thread (see page 21). Hang each one on a jump ring and then on ear clips.

WOOL EARRINGS

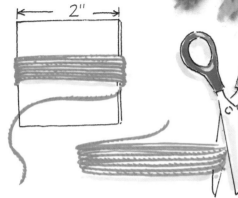

2"

1 Wind lengths of wool, one color at a time, around a piece of stiff cardboard, about 2 inches wide. Cut through the wool, as shown, to make lots of strands.

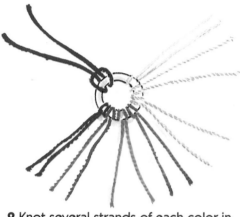

2 Knot several strands of each color in turn around a small curtain ring, as shown. Completely cover the ring with wool strands, pushing the knots together.

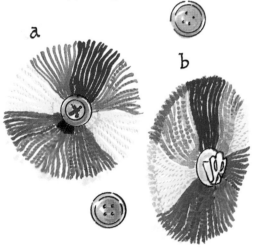

a

b

3 For each earring, sew together two identical flat buttons, one on either side of the curtain ring (a). Glue an ear clip to one of the buttons (b).

TOGGLE BARRETTE

Glue narrow, colored ribbon around the center of three toggles. Glue the toggles on to the middle of a small barrette fittting. Add a brightly colored button or counter on either side.

BUTTON BRACELET

Cut a 7-inch length of wide black elastic. Sew on buttons of all shapes, colors and sizes. Fit them close together, or even overlap them, so that none of the elastic can be seen. Sew the ends of the elastic together to make a colorful button bracelet.

BADGE BRACELET

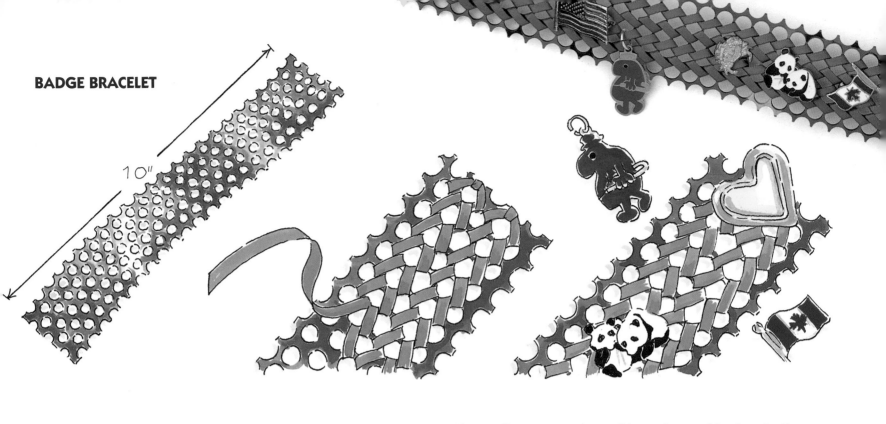

10"

1 Cut a 10-inch length of shiny "honeycomb ribbon." Fold it in half, lengthways, so the holes match, like this.

2 Thread narrow ribbon diagonally through each row of holes. Fold over the ends of the bracelet and sew them down.

3 Pin small brooches and badges to the bracelet. Use the biggest one as a catch to close the bracelet.

SHIRT CUFF BRACELET

Cut the cuff off an old shirt. Using different colored wools, edge it all round with blanket stitch (see page 8). Sew on things like sequins, pompoms, buttons, rings covered in wool, and even an old watch. Sew a small button opposite the buttonhole, so you can close the cuff.

INDEX